You Have

Something

for Everyone

Disclaimer

The information contained in "YOU HAVE SOMETHING FOR EVERYONE" is meant to serve as a comprehensive collection of strategies that the author of this eBook has done research about. Summaries, strategies, tips and tricks are only recommendation by the author, and reading this eBook will not guarantee that one's results will exactly mirror the author's results. The author of the eBook has made all reasonable effort to provide current and accurate information for the readers of the eBook. The author and its associates will not be held liable for any unintentional error or omissions that may be found. The material in the eBook may include information by third parties. Third party materials comprise of opinions expressed by their owners. As such, the author of the eBook does not assume responsibility or liability for any third-party material or opinions. Whether because of the progression of the internet, or the unforeseen changes in company policy and editorial submission guidelines, what is stated as fact at the time of this writing may become outdated or inapplicable later.

The eBook is copyright© 2020 with all rights reserved. It is illegal to redistribute, copy, or create derivative work from this eBook whole or in part. No parts of this report may be reproduced or transmitted in any reproduced or retransmitted in any forms whatsoever without the writing expressed and signed permission from the author of this e-Book.

Copyright© 2020 CHI ANTHONY GUNZ
All rights reserved.

Table of Contents

INTRODUCTION

Value is importance, worth, and usefulness. It is your positive contribution when leaving something better than how you found it. We all have something to contribute to the world. How do I know that? You are here, that's how I know.

You wouldn't be here if you didn't have a special gift to share with the world. Helping others is a fundamental part of humanity. However, sometimes our value is challenging to find. If we do not expose our worth and act on our dreams, then we cannot help anyone.

This book will help you realize your hidden value. First, you will learn that everyone has at least one golden nugget of value hidden inside, and sometimes it takes the encouragement and reinforcement of others believing in them for those golden nuggets to shine.

The purpose of this book is to help you discover and nurture your priceless, hidden golden nuggets of value; what makes you, you!

Follow some of the simple rules in this book, and you will uncover your full potential. You are a gift to the world, a treasure to your family and friends, and an indispensable asset to society. You are a blessing to your parents, siblings, spouse, children, friends, employer, and others. The point is that you have something to share with everyone, and through this book, we will uncover what gifts you have to share with the world.

You serve others by being a good listener and advisor to your friends, talking to your parents who are thrilled to hear your voice, caring for your significant other and your children, as well as handling the upkeep of your home. Your time, advice, services, kindness, and thoughtfulness are all examples of giving to others. Generosity isn't exclusive to the rich; you can give to others without spending money or taking away from your own needs.

Helping others is a great way to spread joy and truly experience the most out of life. Whether you are helping out in your own home or the community, there are endless opportunities to give. Choosing to dedicate time and energy to the betterment of yourself is a noble goal, and may wish to achieve that by improving your health or habits. However, research shows that helping your community and others can lead to greater happiness, less stress, improved pain management, and better overall health.

Pay attention to the people around you and notice little things that you can do to make their lives easier. Even the smallest act of kindness or the simplest gesture can improve someone's day. Be friendly and thoughtful – it is the easiest way to make a significant impact on someone else. Did you know that maintaining good relationships is beneficial for your heart?

YOUR LIFE PURPOSE IS YOUR CONTRIBUTION

Everyone has a unique purpose, but in order to identify and fulfill your purpose, you must put in some hard work and elbow grease.

Some people feel hesitant about pursuing their life purpose because they worry that it sounds like a self-serving or selfish quest. However, true purpose requires you to recognize your values and use them to contribute to the world, whether those gifts are playing beautiful music for others to enjoy, helping friends solve problems, or simply bringing more joy into the lives of those around you. The first thing you need is an introduction to you. You need to know everything about yourself to identify what you can offer others that aligns with your values. Only then can you begin to hone in on what is or isn't an opportunity for you. In this book, you will learn how to find the nuggets of gold inside of you, and how to make them benefit everyone around you.

Everyone shares a responsibility to become self-aware, so we can further use what we have to help others and fulfill our purpose. From this practice, we can also solve our issues and problems more effectively. So, the practice of self-awareness is essential in every way. This book will help you to identify the skills you need to set life goals, enhance your employability prospects, raise your confidence, and lead to a more fulfilling and higher quality life by providing others what they need. It will enable you to learn how to make relevant, positive, and productive decisions for your future and enable personal empowerment.

Before you start the journey to reveal the uncommon things that make you unique, you must take time to become aware of your potential. Take a half-day retreat to reflect on what makes you special, what you value, and what skills you'd like to offer others. Ask yourself questions about your unique qualities, things you admire, and things you naturally excel in. By answering these questions, you will be able to uncover possibilities for your work. True purpose points to the end of a self-

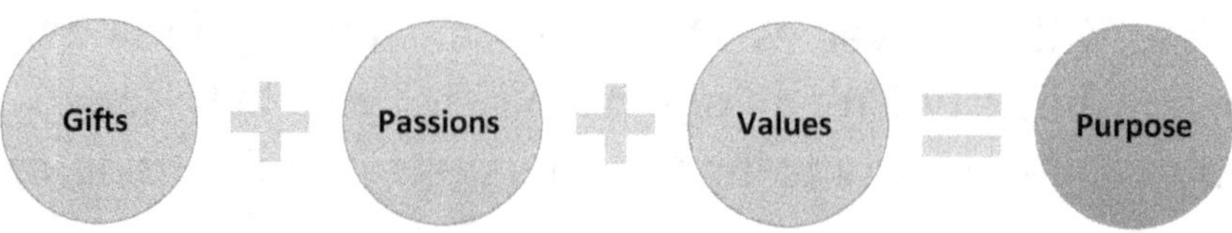

absorbed, self-serving relationship to life. When your authentic purpose becomes clear, you will be able to share it with the whole world. The equation for purpose is G + P + V = P. **(Gifts + Passions + Values = Purpose) Richard Leider**

Your life purpose consists of the central motivating aims of your life, the reasons you get up in the morning. Purpose can guide life decisions, influence behavior, shape goals, offer a sense of direction and create meaning. Your life purpose consists of the central motivating factors of your life. For some people, purpose connects directly with a passion for their work. For others, purpose lies in their responsibilities to family or friends. Others seek meaning through spirituality or religious beliefs. Some people may find their purpose clearly expressed in all these aspects of life. Purpose will be unique for everyone; what you identify as your path will be different than others. What's more, your purpose can shift and change throughout life in response to your own experiences and evolving priorities. Questions that may come up when you reflect upon your life purpose are:

Questioning/Answering Section

- Who am I?
- Where do I belong?
- What am I good at doing?
- When do I feel fulfilled?
- Where am I vulnerable?
- Where do I need to improve?
- What opportunities are available?
- Do I have something for others?
- What skills do I struggle to master?
- Are there factors beyond my control?
- Which things I can share with others?
- What do I want?
- Why is it so hard to find my life purpose?
- What do I want to achieve in this world?
- How would I behave if I did have this skill/trait?
- Have some factors made an impact on my goals?
- If this is not how I like it: how would I like it to be?
- What do other people most often identify as my weakness?
- Are there one or two aspects of my personality that hold you back?
- What sort of impact on others do I hope to make doing what I do?

- ❖ If this situation was the way I wanted it to be, how would it look, sound, or feel?
- ❖ Given all the resources I needed to change this, what changes would I make?
- ❖ What do I do, only to satisfy job requirements?
- ❖ Where do I lack experience, resources, or connections, where others have them?

Find Your Reason To Live

Finding and realizing your reason to live will not happen overnight. By working toward your reason to live over time, you will continue to grow and develop in your chosen field or profession. Your life is your choice, so you can feel a sense of autonomy over the journey it takes to get there. Your reason to live is often not grand or extraordinary, making it approachable and realistic to achieve. In that way, having a goal improves your well-being because you are always working toward something meaningful. When you feel that you have an adequate sense of yourself, brainstorm a few things that could be your reason to live. Then ask yourself what you need to start and stop doing to get there.

Claim Your Values

Start by making a list of everything you value, or use this list of common core values for inspiration. Then, narrow that list down to five of your most deeply held values. Looking at your list, think about how your current life and work support and reflect these values. How do they show up for you daily? What examples do you have of times when you have truly lived your values? Think about which values you may be ignoring or not giving enough attention to in your current situation. How can you bring more attention to these values and how you can share these with others? What do you need to start or stop doing to embrace and live these values fully? Your values represent who you are at your core. When you deeply understand and claim your values, decisions become easier to make, and you can start putting your dreams into action. Find out what you are willing to make sacrifices to achieve. You sacrifice to the point of burnout. When you find something that you are willing to sacrifice a lot for, you know that you have found your purpose. So, ask yourself: what are you willing to sacrifice for?

SELF-AWARENESS

Know yourself; know your worth. Self-awareness allows you to recognize what things you do best so you can find aspects of your life. It also helps you accept your weaknesses. Self-awareness is your ability to accept your weaknesses while focusing all of your attention on your strengths. The moment you decide to accept your shortcomings and bet entirely on your strengths, things will change. You only need to believe in yourself. Typically, humans like to avoid pain. Realizing that beyond fear and pain lies freedom, possibility, and healing is the first step in the right direction. We have positives & negatives and everything in between. Self-awareness requires seeing the truth for what it is. In some cases, the truth hurts.

EFFECT OF YOUR PERSONALITY ON OTHERS

You must be aware of the value of being positive and upbeat so that it can influence everyone around you and combat your negativity. For example, a friendly smile to a stranger can brighten up their day, just as a glare can cause their mood to drop. So, your aim in life is to be a good human being and to make others happy not to make them feel worse or ashamed.

Putting a smile on someone's face is a great feeling.

The following traits will benefit others: *your love, your trust & loyalty, your time, your advice, your services, your kindness, your excellent communication, your honesty, your technical competency, your work ethic, your flexibility to a situation, your determination, persistence, and ability to do others work, etc.*

This book will find essential and significant points about how to find your inner values and how to boost personal growth. This book will help you identify the skills that you need to set life goals, which can increase your employability prospects and wealth, raise your confidence, and lead to a more fulfilling, higher quality life. Self-improvement gives you wings, with the help of your wings, you can fly higher in life and get everything that you planned for yourself. Plan to make relevant, positive, and productive life choices and decisions for your future to enable personal empowerment.

Become The Best Possible Version of Yourself.

While you may not be able to help it if you are having a bad day or don't like doing a particular task, changing your attitude changes everything, complaining and sulking will only make time drag when doing an unpleasant job. Instead, try to shift your thoughts and redirect your mind. Being a more pleasant person helps everyone.

BELIEVE IN YOURSELF

The ability to believe in yourself can change your life, open up a lot of opportunities in your life, and it is essential in improving your personality. Sometimes you have to face many challenging tasks. The reality is that you doubt yourself, but you must re-train yourself. By this, you can get rid of all your fears and self-doubts, and you will be able to build self-esteem and self-confidence. The primary key is to be sincere with yourself and live your life full of aspirations.

Many scientists believe that the human mind is influenced by the outside world. The mind is such a strong and powerful tool that can deliver everything you want through positive expectations. With a positive attitude, you can expect to achieve what you want in life. It is a game of the mind that revolves around your choice and discipline. You must specify some time to think about who you are and what you believe in and what is valuable to you.

You can have everything you want to be in your life as a result of belief in yourself, and you have to believe that it's not impossible. Don't forget that you always have a lot of choices. To believe in yourself, you first have to believe that what you want is possible. Practice the following steps to begin believing in yourself.

Believe Nothing Is Impossible

You have to believe that you can do anything. If you want to develop your personality, it is possible. You do not need to worry about what people think or say about you and where you stand in your life because everything is possible for you. By believing in yourself, you will find the courage to take immediate action on your goals. And this, as you may know, is the key to success!

Understanding personality traits is a great way to start your journey toward self-discovery. Make a concerted effort to fill up that journal with evocative questions and answers. Invest and mold yourself into the best possible version of yourself. If you're up for the challenge, you can make positive changes to your personality based on a deep understanding of yourself and others.

Start With Creating Your Personality

No one but you can create your personality. It encompasses the actions you take and the decisions you make. Either you are a patient person or not, a responsible person, or not. Try asking yourself some searching questions to discover just what kind of person you are.

There are many different personality types. Your personality factors will help you gain more insight into your  internal experience to make sense of your thoughts and behaviors. You may not be able to change your personality type, but you can change aspects of your personality by taking determined, active steps to become a more balanced person. Taking up a hobby is a great way to become a well-rounded individual. Sports can help you learn teamwork, arts and crafts can make you more patient, volunteering can help you become more caring. Even just reading a book can expand your horizons and push you to be better.

HOW TO BECOME SELF-AWARE

Improving who you are and how you feel about yourself will result in positive progress toward your goal. Becoming self-aware means that you are living life proactively, taking control, and learning about yourself in the process. Through self-awareness, you can become who want to be and who you are meant to become. Here are some steps to have a self-aware personality.

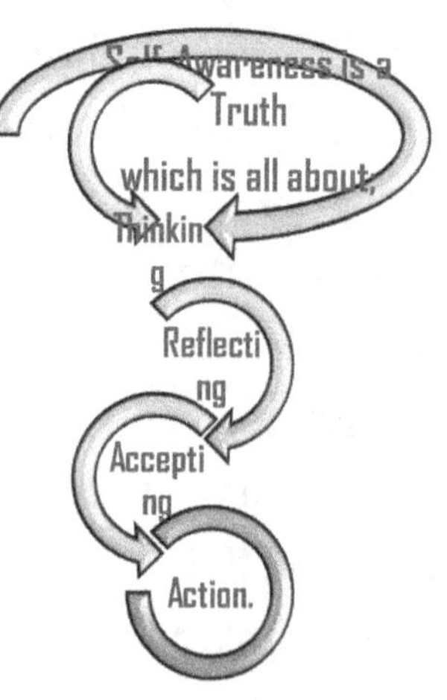

- ❖ Know your strengths and weaknesses
- ❖ Recall your natural strengths and interests
- ❖ Collect all resources
- ❖ Ask yourself the questions related to yourself
- ❖ Learn from your mistakes
- ❖ Try new things
- ❖ Get free time for yourself
- ❖ Think about yourself
- ❖ Become aware of your behaviors

❖ Analyze your personality by taking a test

KNOW YOUR STRENGTHS & WEAKNESSES:

You can ask others about your strengths and weaknesses as they can offer an objective perspective. The objective view of others can be extremely enlightening and informative when analyzing our personality. You have to assess yourself with the help of others. Once you come to know about your strengths and weaknesses, you can work out on them.

RECALL YOUR NATURAL STRENGTHS & INTERESTS:

Think back to your childhood and recall your talents. If you are unable to remember your childhood strengths, you can get help from the people who are close to you. Ask those you trust about yourself and about your life. Ask them about any stories, observations, or clues that could give you insight into yourself and who you are. Make sure this is done in a space where the other person feels safe.

❖ What were you good at?
❖ What were your interests?
❖ What were your capabilities?
❖ What were you naturally drawn to?

COLLECT ALL RESOURCES:

Once you realize your strengths and weaknesses, now it's time to make them according to your goals. You have to set, analyze, and improve them for better results. Gather the resources and knowledge needed to help you address these areas. Utilize available resources like books, videos, courses, podcasts, mentors, notebooks, pencils, and paper, etc. So, you can accelerate learning. Learn from the mistakes of others. Just because others make them doesn't mean you have to.

ASK YOURSELF THE QUESTIONS RELATED TO YOURSELF:

You must give yourself permission to be courageous, face your fears, and solve drawbacks. One should be able to answer questions related to one's likes/dislikes, motivators/downers, preferences, habits/patterns, etc. You can quiz yourself by asking a lot of questions. You can ask questions like:

* What are my best/worst qualities?
* What are my goals, beliefs, values?
* How would I respond if ___________?
* What would I do if ________________?
* Could I deal with _____________ situation?
* What is stopping me from _______________?

LEARN FROM YOUR MISTAKES:

Humans make mistakes and no one is perfect, but mistakes can actually be beneficial. The ability to learn from your mistakes and admit your faults is priceless. First, you must admit that you made a mistake and then you can begin to learn from that mistake as to not repeat it in the future. The nature of your mistakes can also be informative in becoming self-aware. Self-awareness is lifelong learning. You can ask yourself the following questions:

- ❖ What happened?
- ❖ What did I do well?
- ❖ Where did I go wrong?
- ❖ What can I do next time?
- ❖ What could I have done better?

YOU MUST TRY NEW THINGS:

Learn new things. Have new experiences. Embrace new opportunities. Trying new things means going outside of your comfort zone. Going outside this zone doesn't mean taking huge steps, you can start small. Little changes and decisions will do the trick. Opportunities exist, find them. If nothing is available, create opportunities for yourself. No one is going to work for you, so you have to step up.

GET FREE TIME FOR YOURSELF:

Set aside some time for yourself, by improving yourself. Small amounts of time spent on improvement compounded over the course of days, weeks, and years will radically change your life. Take time and build up from there. Improve yourself on the spot, no need to not wait for the "best time." You have to believe it's the best time to do something, or else you will never improve.

THINK ABOUT YOURSELF:

As outside resources and other people will help you become more self-aware, you ultimately need to determine who you are by yourself. External input is great and has its place, but nothing beats your own perspective, insight, and feelings.

BECOME AWARE OF YOUR BEHAVIORS:

An important step is to know your moods. If you feel mood swings, you must deal with it immediately. Your attitude towards something can affect the final result. Ask yourself scenario questions. Detach yourself from your emotions. Reflect in the 3rd person. Reflect on past tendencies. If you isolate yourself, become impatient, have decision fatigue, lack a filter, become frustrated, procrastinate, overeat, become lazy, stubborn, look inward, read, watch movies, don't speak and argue about things, it is the result of your inner weaknesses. You need to figure out how you have responded to situations, problems, and normal day-to-day living.

ANALYZE YOUR PERSONALITY BY TAKING A TEST:

There are many ways to analyze your personality. You can do it by yourself, you can get help from your relatives, you can even use an app to analyze your personality or any other useful tool.

MIND SET UP TO HELP OTHERS

The mindset is the key to changing your fortune. It's how you go from average results to a healthy and wealthy life. Your mindset is the framework of your mind. It is the sum of all opinions, options, beliefs, and thoughts. These things make a separate world inside you. There are many examples of people with a helping mindset. They achieved everything through their hard work. They have gone on to make amazing things out of themselves. The sportsman in the playground, the teacher in school, or any Individuals with a success mindset always lead themselves to make things happen in the real world and give colors to dreams without noticing the impossible things. As you've seen the leaders who've managed to resolve all unbelievable circumstances and issues which a country has to face have a thought and belief system known as the success mindset.

Your mindset is a fixed state of mind. You have your mind as an empty box and want to fill that box with everything that makes you the person that you are. How will that work if you are not going to change yourself? Determine how you perceive and react to special events. Right now, it is very useful to have a helping mindset because it's all about what you want from your life. It makes you be flexible to weigh different decisions in life. It also enables you to do your job best in order to achieve whatever you want from your life.

A mindset is the sum of all opinions, options, beliefs, and thoughts that shape your thought habits and your daily routines. It impacts how you feel about  your surroundings and the world around you. You may not believe that this would be easy to change, but it is. Your mindsets are strongly ingrained in your beliefs and thoughts. They need extra attention in order to change them. Your mindset is a fixed state of mind that can interpret situations and determine your response. It also filters reality in front of you. You are able to create positive results instead of negative consequences. Mindsets can change, but they tend to change slowly. It's very easy and simple to correct our attitude towards personal development. Your mindset creates a short-term reaction called an attitude. It is an arranged way of thinking or feeling about someone or something specific.

If you really motivated to find your values, you must set your mind according to your desire.

YOU HAVE THINGS FOR EVERYONE

The trend in our society is for people to be separated from each other, to be cut off from the great mass of humanity, and in doing so to be dehumanized a little bit more with each step. Society is moving towards selfishness rather than helping our brothers and sisters in humanity. Helping or giving something to a fellow human being, while it can be inconvenient, has a few humble advantages; It makes you feel better about yourself; It connects you with another person, at least for a moment, if not for life; It improves the life of another, at least a little; It makes the world a better place, one baby step at a time and if that kindness is passed on, it can multiply exponentially. So, take just a few minutes today, and do something kind for another person. It can be something small, or the start of something big. There a lot of things which you can share with others and make them happy. If you think you will find a lot of ways to do this, continue to brainstorm more ways:

1. **Smile for everyone**

2. **Be friendly with others**

3. Love others

4. Respect others

5. Encourage others

6. Be Honest to others

7. Be loyal to others

8. Have compassion for others

9. Help friends and family

10. Forgive others

11. Service others

12. Be patient to others

13. Have flexibility for others

14. Say thank you to others

15. Congratulate others on their special events

16. Comfort others in grief

17. Volunteer for others

18. Donate something to charity

19. Stop and help the needy

20. Teach good things to others

21. Help and care for the poor

22.Help someone who is on the edge

23.Help someone to get active

24.Listen to others

25.Accept others as they are

26.Give gifts to others which you can afford

27.Inspire a positive attitude in others

SMILE FOR EVERYONE

A smile is the most natural and powerful gift we possess. Sometimes a simple little thing like a smile can give a smile and warm feeling to someone else and make their day a little better. They might then do the same for others. On top of spreading love and happiness, by making people smile more you are also helping them lead healthier lives. Inflammation on the cellular level caused by stress has been a known risk factor for cell mutation and diseases like cancer.

Have you observed what happens when someone smiles? Have you ever seen a newborn baby smiling? If yes, I wager that it is the most beautiful thing one has ever experienced. Yes, that is the power of smiling. It gives endless positivity in your life. Countless scientific studies have confirmed that a genuine smile is generally considered attractive to others around us. Try to have a smile on your face all the time. It will relax you and inspire others around you to also smile.

- ❖ Smiling relieves stress
- ❖ Smiling makes us attractive
- ❖ Smiling makes us feel good
- ❖ Smiling elevates our mood
- ❖ Smiling helps you stay positive
- ❖ Smiling makes you look younger
- ❖ Smiling lowers your blood pressure
- ❖ Smiling makes you seem successful
- ❖ Smiling boosts your immune system

BE FRIENDLY WITH OTHERS

When you give your best attention to people expressing thoughts and experiences that are important to them, those individuals are likely to see you as someone who cares about their well-being. This fact is especially true when you give your attention only and refrain from interjecting opinions, judgments, and advice. This makes you friendly to them. Being friendly with others is something very beautiful. Think about a time when someone was friendly to you. Maybe drawing you into a gathering, saying hello on the sidewalk, or smiling from across the room. How did you feel? Probably more included, comfortable, and at ease, safe and sound, more open and warm-hearted.

When you are friendly to others, you offer them the same benefits and you also get rewarded. Being friendly encourages others to be less guarded or reactive with you. Supporting someone can be really hard but you have a mindset to do something, believe that it's not impossible. It showed that calmness and understanding are the only healthy options you have when you're confronted with someone who's dealing with underlying pain. Here are some of the advantages of being friendly with others:

- ❖ It makes them feel good.
- ❖ It will likely come back to you.
- ❖ You'll strengthen their willpower.
- ❖ Good deeds add meaning to their life.
- ❖ You can make a difference with friendliness.

Having Love For Others

Love is something that every person desires. Everyone has their own definition of love because it is a feeling that comes from within, but the general feeling of love is simply a fondness or appreciation for someone. It's the best thing you can have for somebody. Simply find ways to express your love to others, whether it be your partner, child, another family member, friend, co-worker, or a complete stranger. A hug, a kind word, spending time, showing little kindnesses, and being friendly are all ways to show love. You can't help who you fall in love with. It is not right to make people feel uncomfortable about who they are just because some people do not agree with them. Not everyone is going to agree all the time. If everyone was the same way the world would be boring because there would not be any diversity.

Love is a healthy emotional attachment in relationships between friends and family members. Everyone should love and be loved by someone. Remember that love is not only for couples. Loving others shows a deep connection to the people around us. When we love others, we can encourage them to heal their pain, develop support, and discover empathy. Our ability to love others reveals inspiring humanity in us. It's all about respecting others without expecting the same from them. Love is one of the many gifts of life that everyone should have the ability to experience. I feel as though people should not have to be afraid to be who they are. Examples of loving others can include honoring, trusting, and valuing them. Saying a kind word to someone who puts themselves down can transform their psyche, leaving a lasting impact on them. Loving others creates healing, as we break away from addiction and its stigmas into core change.

HAVING RESPECT FOR OTHERS

Receiving respect is essential for others because it helps others to feel safe and to express themselves. It is a necessary component of healthy relationships. Respect, as an act of love for others, can include encouraging and supporting others to maintain sobriety. Support is one of the most critical elements of healing and growth. Respect is the glue that holds your relationships together. When someone's love struggles with darker moments, you can provide encouragement and support by actively listening, showing compassion and empathy, and asking how you can help. You can additionally express your gratitude for a friend, family member, or recovery peer, respecting their being and nurturing your relationships.

Respect comes with embracing acceptance, not judging others, valuing others' viewpoints, actively listening, having forgiveness, showing compassion, and appreciating each other's personalities. When you respect each other, you can see the value they have to offer with an openness to their core being. When you listen to others, for example, you value what they have to say. You can relate to them as you give them your attention.

We live in a world where there are many differences between people. With an open mind and an appreciation of each person's contributions to this world, we strengthen our relationships and our community.

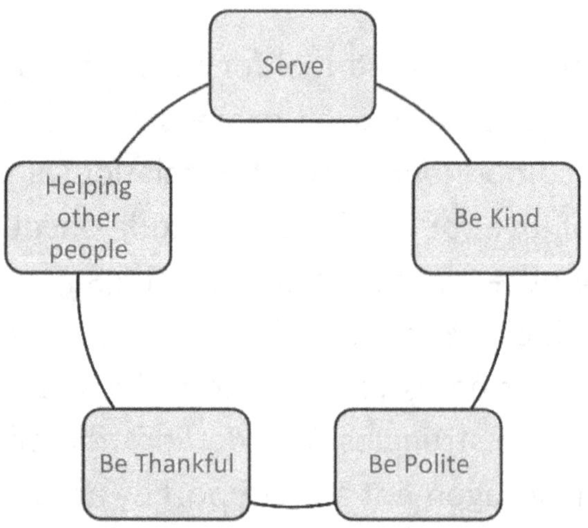

So, everyone must make it a habit to look for the unique talents of each person we meet and be respectful of their differences. If you want your relationships to be harmonious, just remember two basic guidelines for success: mutual respect and gratitude. If you're looking to improve your relationships with others, try these easy ways to show your appreciation and respect.

Coaching and providing people an opportunity to increase their knowledge and skills is an excellent task you can do. You can respect others' growth by respecting and valuing all questions. There is no such thing as a dumb question. Furthermore, you respect others by asking them what you can do to help them grow and improve.

1. Respecting others who are experiencing difficulties. You can show this type of respect in various ways, but offer to help them with tasks that may be difficult to complete during their hardship.

2. Listening actively and really showing appreciation When someone has something important to say. It is so meaningful to know someone else truly cares about and is interested in you. That is respect, and it has a significant effect on the relationship. Listening can be one of the hardest skills to master. If you want a person to know you respect him or her, then tune into what that person is saying. Look them in the eye, put down your cell phone, and offer feedback when necessary. Everyone appreciates the person who willingly listens to them and shows genuine interest in what they have to say.

HAVING ENCOURAGEMENT FOR OTHERS

Encouragement is the act of giving someone support, confidence, and hope. Even if you know that everyone needs encouragement, not everyone is willing to give it. The selfishness of human nature makes it easy to judge others or put them down. In a world where challenges abound, it's easy for you to feel discouraged. But realize that if you've ever had a bad day, you know the power a little encouragement can have. We all have moments when we need someone to tell us, "Don't worry! Everything will work out." It might not seem like much at the time, but that person will remember that you took an interest in their feelings and well-being. A smile and uplifting word can truly brighten someone's day. Here are some ways to encourage others.

- ❖ Help them
- ❖ Share with others
- ❖ Show them you care
- ❖ Tell them in writing
- ❖ Trust them with more
- ❖ Realize the power of presence
- ❖ Be specific when you offer words of praise
- ❖ Let people know that you're praying for them
- ❖ Make celebration a regular part of your relationships

There are many benefits for others if you encourage them, like:

- ❖ It gives others hope.
- ❖ It helps to build self-esteem.
- ❖ It helps to restore self-confidence.
- ❖ It helps them to change their perspective.
- ❖ It provides energy to accomplish their objective.

❖ It helps to make people work harder and get succeed.

1) It gives others hope.

When people are at their lowest level of hope, they tend to withdraw from other people because they fear their judgment. But if you can empower them with encouragement, you will bring them hope. That hope will motivate them to take one small step after another until they see the brightness of better days.

2) It helps to build self-esteem.

Your words of encouragement can help make people feel good about themselves. One of the most important things they need to know as they face the harsh realities of life is that you will be there to support them with words of encouragement. Nothing is impossible for them if they try it.

3) It helps to restore self-confidence.

Encouragement is more than a confidence booster. It is also a show of faith that other people support that individual.

4) It helps them to change their perspective.

When they are in the middle of trials and challenges, they can get confused. It can lead them to view things differently. It can sometimes point their focus on immediate things. Their desire to survive makes them unable to see the big picture, and it often leads them to make wrong decisions. Your encouragement can help to calm them and make them pause and analyze what's going on in their life. It has the power to make them see the situation from a better perspective.

5) *It provides energy to accomplish their objective.* Words of encouragement work like energy pills that can give a person the strength that he/she need to overcome the obstacles that lay between them and their objectives. It is a light in the tunnel that gives them hope, knowing that there's someone who believes that they can make it.

6) *It helps to make people work harder and get succeed.*

Encouragement makes people work harder to finish a task because they know there is someone who can guide them on the right path of success. They believe in you if you provide them with the encouragement which they desperately needed. Encouragement is a great motivator.

HAVING HONESTY FOR OTHERS

Honesty is the bridge to authenticity and self-compassion. Openness allows you to set realistic goals. It bolsters your courage and frees you to be your best self. Simplicity in life cannot be achieved without honesty. Honesty can live without simplicity, but simplicity cannot live without honesty. Consider the fact that every time you are not truthful, you create an alternate reality. And subsequently, you are forced to live a life in both worlds: the true one and the one you've created. When you choose honesty in all aspects of life, including your marriage, business, and relationships, you live the same life as you are. Honesty leads to simplicity, but dishonesty leads to duplicity. Being honest with yourself and with others shows how much you care.

- ❖ A caring attitude makes people stop and think.
- ❖ Gentle honesty is also very attractive and appealing.
- ❖ It also demonstrates self-respect and respect for others.
- ❖ Honesty can bring people closer by creating a safe connection.
- ❖ If you want people to know who you really are, be honest in your self-expression.
- ❖ If honesty becomes an unconscious habit, you will become very attractive to other honest people. A life filled with authentic people is vastly enriched.

The following are many other benefits of being honest:

Benefits Of Being Honest

- It fosters courage.
- It shows you care.
- It eliminates garbage.
- It fosters a connection.
- It promotes authenticity.
- Honesty attracts honesty.
- It can keep you out of trouble.
- It shows maturity and self-acceptance.
- It feels exhilarating because it is so freeing.

HAVING LOYALTY FOR OTHERS

Loyalty is the best thing you can give to someone. A loyal relationship has the chance to last forever. Being loyal to those around you can be a challenge, as it requires patience and generosity. A person that shows loyalty to you does so with no personal agenda. It is pure selflessness in a sense to where they put your needs over their own. Loyalty is the ability to put others before yourself and stick with them in good times and bad. Show commitment to friends, family, and significant others by being honest, trustworthy, supportive, and generous. Maintain healthy boundaries with those around you so you can be loyal to them in a productive way.

Employers want and need to trust their employees to work professionally to meet the employer's best interests. Employers do not want to hire people who require scrutiny or cannot be trusted to represent the company. Loyalty is also incredibly important because it can be rare. No matter if the person you are trying to be more loyal to is right or wrong, you have their back. Especially when they are called out about it. It doesn't matter if you agree with their decision or would have done the total opposite. Stand by their side when no one else will. That is loyalty. So, when people get it from you, they will follow you to the end of the earth. They will respect you so much more, and you will build loyalty with them. Here are five ways to be a genuinely loyal person in a relationship:

- ❖ Be sincere
- ❖ Be respectful
- ❖ Have integrity
- ❖ Be supportive
- ❖ Be trustworthy

There are three methods to be loyal with others.

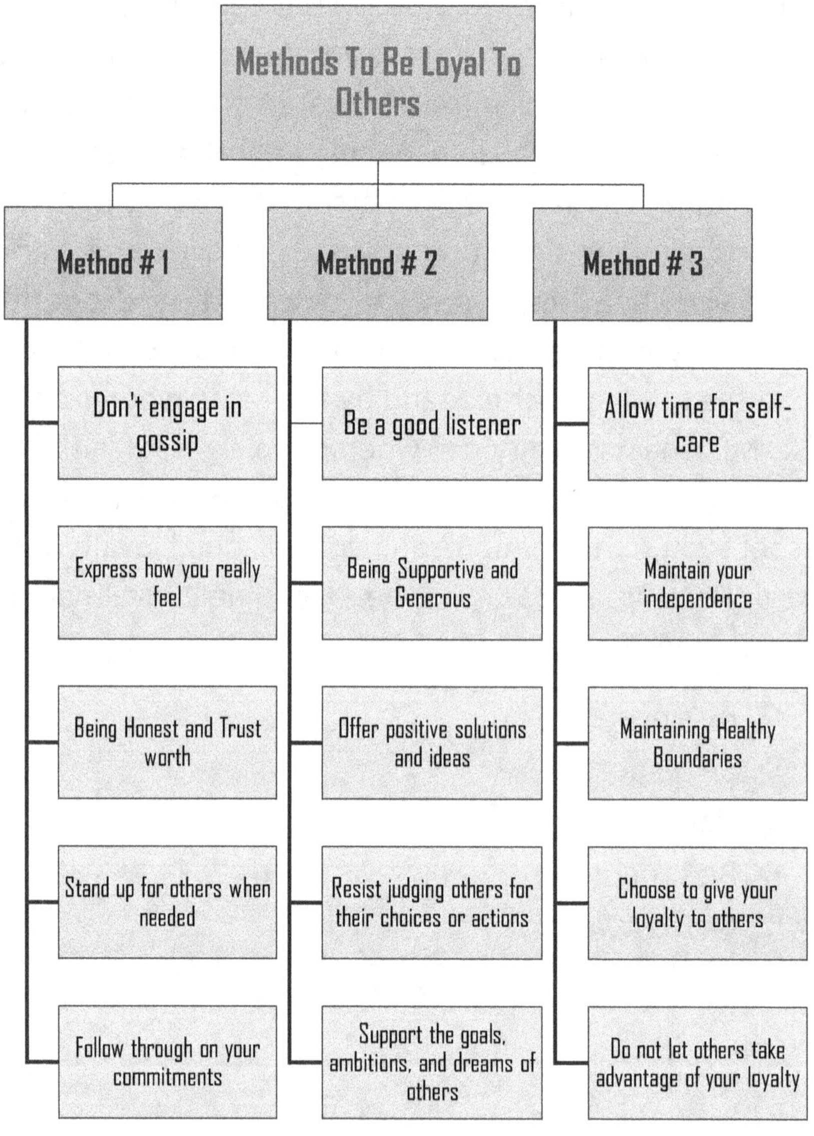

HAVING COMPASSION FOR OTHERS

We all need compassion because life is hard. We are all susceptible to diseases and injuries. Every one of us has a lifespan that had a start and will have an end. Life experiences can also diminish our ability to give and receive compassion. Having compassion for others allows you to empathize with them and see yourself in them. Empathy is the kindness and sympathy you have for yourself and other people. Empathy is an act of healing that can help alleviate pain and encourage others to heal. Compassion reminds you that we human beings are all doing the very best we can despite our adversities.

Compassion enables you to release anger and unnecessary conflicts with the understanding that people change and make mistakes. You are still human, and accepting who you are, regardless of where you are from, is central to feeling and expressing compassion for others. This list of 10 different ways to show compassion, one for each letter of the word, is composed of easy ways that people of all ages can try to show compassion during this season, or better yet in everyday life, regardless of the time.

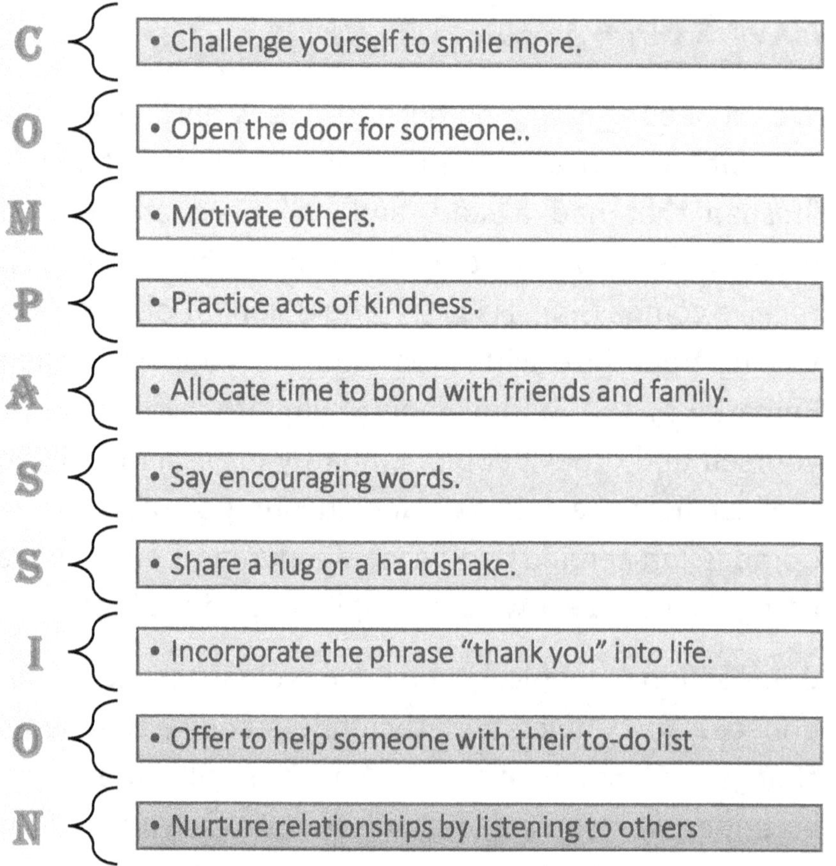

1. *Challenge yourself to smile more.*

Most of the time, people are just neutral. Challenge yourself to smile more. Smile at everyone around you. Changing your look from unemotive to something more like the "happy smiley face" is a small action that can have a significant impact on someone else.

2. *Open the door for someone.*

Think about the last time someone held a door open for you. Maybe it was at a store when your hands were full of shopping bags. Perhaps it was as you were entering or exiting school. No matter where it took place, chances are you were grateful to the person who held the door for you because it was one less task you had to worry about as you were moving to your next destination. Take a few seconds to open the door for someone else, and better yet, remember to smile as they walk by you.

3. *Motivate others.*

Motivation is often a concept that many people struggle with. With help from others, encouraging words and positivity can help to uplift someone's spirit. Use some of these key phrases to help in your motivation.

4. *Practice acts of kindness.*

Many activities are considered acts of kindness. Attempt to practice at least two different acts of kindness a day. Maybe donate clothes to the poor, help serve meals in a soup kitchen, or take a minute to hold the door open for someone else.

5. *Allocate time to bond with friends and family.*

Life is too short to be "busy" all the time. We all tend to get caught up in the daily hustle and bustle of getting done all the chores around the inside of the house and outside the home. Set aside time to forget about everything you need to do and spend a few hours catching up with family and friends. It will be time well spent, and you will have plenty of time to catch up on your to-do list later.

6. *Say encouraging words.*

Today's world is full of negativity. You have to keep a positive attitude and need to develop it in others as well. It seems that nothing is ever good enough, and the things people do often come up short of perfect. Instead of dwelling on everything people do wrong, use your voice to tell them what they are doing right and encourage them to continue working towards their goals.

7. *Share a hug or a handshake.*

The power of touch is unique. Sharing a hug or a handshake can be a powerful but simple way to show compassion. Try to utilize hugs and handshakes in a variety of situations to show others that you care.

8. *Incorporate the phrase "thank you" into life.*

As you know, manners matter a lot! We often believe that our gratefulness for any given act is understood, but the reality of the situation is that our thankfulness for most things in life is left unspoken. Try to say "thank you" in more of your routine activities. Gratitude is something that should never be left unspoken.

9. *Offer to help someone with their to-do list.*

To-do lists seem endless; however, as the saying goes, many hands make light work—volunteer to help someone out with his or her chore list. Checking any task off that list will feel like a great accomplishment.

10. *Nurture relationships by listening to others.*

Sometimes, the easiest way to build a relationship can be done simply by listening. Contribute to the conversation, but try not to take it over. It is easy to be the only person talking in a situation, and it is much more challenging to listen to others' contributions.

HELPING FRIENDS AND FAMILY

Talk to a family member or friend and ask what they most need help with and offer your services. By offering before they need to ask you, you are showing that you care about them. Remember to follow through with whatever they've asked of you. Simply asking won't help them. Make a routine of questioning around your circle of friends and family for what they need—before long, assisting others to will simply be second nature to you! Often what people need is simply someone who will listen to them with kindness and without judgment.

When someone is telling you about themselves, or a hardship they are going through, don't merely leap in with your feelings, thoughts, and stories. Practice active listening. When you're listening to someone, stay focused on what they are saying. Look at the speaker and let go of distracting thoughts. If your mind wanders, the other person will notice, and they won't feel like you are paying attention. Do something like, make a meal and bring it over to their house during a particularly busy or stressful time, so they don't have to worry about feeding themselves. This is a particularly kind thing to do for someone who has just had a loved one die or become seriously ill. When someone is busy or stressed, chores and jobs often slip through the cracks. Find out from your family and friends what they're too busy or stressed to do and set aside some time to do it for them.

HAVING FORGIVENESS FOR OTHERS

Forgiveness puts the final seal on what happened that hurt you. It's a process over time that includes letting go of negative emotions, thoughts, and behaviors, and replacing those with positive thoughts, feelings, and actions toward the offender. Much of our pain in life comes from not being able to forgive and forget what someone may have said or done. If you are in emotional or even physical pain, forgiveness could be the answer you have been seeking.

The most important thing you can give others is to forgive him/her for all their mistakes. Maybe they made all their mistakes intently, but perhaps it was due to involuntary actions. Forgiveness is inextricably intertwined with self-development and spiritual growth, and it plays a pivotal role in the formation and maintenance of healthy relationships. Happy people are more forgiving than unhappy people, and there is a significant correlation between forgiveness and health, especially concerning stress. Forgiveness is proven to reduce stress levels and increase levels of happiness. It's a gift you give to yourself.

Forgiveness has been associated with spiritual and emotional healing since the dawn of humanity. Of course, forgiving someone who has hurt you is harder than it sounds. In forgiveness, one overcomes criticism, anger, hatred, blame, frustration, resentment, hostility, rumination, revenge, and other negative feelings, thoughts, and behaviors in a healthy manner. When you forgive those nagging, negative thoughts, they will go away. Research shows that you'll most likely experience less fear, anger, and depression - not to mention improved sleep, less physical pain, better cardiac function, and increased life satisfaction. Forgiveness has also been impressive is psychology and neuroscience.

Researchers show that there is a set of processes between brain structure and function that allows a person to think and feel in ways that promote forgiveness. By forgiving others, we create stronger relationships and encourage bonds as we grow and understand one another. When you practice forgiveness, you can show others love by choosing to be understanding of their faults and messy pasts and open to growing with them in new ways. Forgiveness reveals love for others and reflects a maturity in sustaining connections with people as they evolve. It is time to stop dwelling on what happened. By forgiving someone, you promise not to bring it up again to use it against him or her. If you are going to talk to someone about how the other person has hurt you, make sure this person is a professional or a wise person you can trust. When you stop judging and simply become an observer, you will know inner peace. With that sense of inner peace, you will find yourself happier and free of the negative energy of resentment. Most of us hold at least some misconceptions about forgiveness. Here are some things that forgiving someone doesn't mean:

1. Forgiveness isn't something you do for the other person.
2. Forgiveness doesn't mean you should forget the incident ever happened.
3. Forgiveness doesn't mean you have to continue to include the person in your life.

4. Forgiveness doesn't mean you need to tell the person that he or she is forgiven.
5. Forgiveness doesn't mean you shouldn't have any more feelings about the situation.
6. Forgiveness doesn't mean you are pardoning or excusing the other person's actions.
7. Forgiveness doesn't mean there is nothing further to work out in the relationship or that everything is okay now.

If you decide, you are willing to forgive, find a good place, and time to be alone with your thoughts. Then, try following these four steps to forgive even when it feels impossible:

1. Think about the incident that angered you. Accept that it happened. Accept how you felt about it and how it made you react.
2. Acknowledge the growth you experienced as a result of what happened.
3. Now think about the other person. He or she is flawed because all human beings are flawed. He or she acted from limited beliefs and a skewed frame of reference because sometimes we all act from our limited beliefs and skewed frames of reference. When you were hurt, the other person was trying

to have a need met. Think why this was a need for him/her?

4. Finally, decide whether or not you want to tell the other person that you have forgiven him or her. If you decide not to express forgiveness directly, then do it on your own. Say the words, "I forgive you," aloud and then add as much explanation as you feel is merited.

BE A SERVICE TO OTHERS

The best thing you can do for yourself and the people of this planet is to be of service to others. You don't have to quit your job and give up your life to join volunteers in a remote area to help disaster victims or donate your life savings to charity. You don't have to work at a food bank or with at-risk teens unless you want to. Being of service to others allows us to love them by helping them when in need. Volunteering our time to others will enable us to recognize that we are works in progress while connecting to the development that others are trying to make. Helping others can make us happy, reduce stress, and build community. Assisting others also keeps us humble as we put others' needs before our own, reducing depression and enhancing self-esteem. Being of service is not only about what you do, but also about how you do it. True service means that you are doing what is expected of you, and doing it with compassion and love.

Understanding that service is both attitude and action helps you to see that the opportunities for being of service are constant in everything you do. The amazing thing about serving others and giving is that it positively affects the giver. You can't give to others without also reaping benefits yourself. When you see yourself as a servant leader, you will never lack for an audience to help. Remember that wherever you are in life, there is still someone you can help somehow. When you look for ways to help others, you'll find that you are constantly blessed with things. Encourage others, stop to hear what people are saying to you, put yourself in the other person's shoes, think before you speak, and above all, put on love as your top priority whenever you interact with others. You can use your services as inspiration to find ways to give back. Here are some services you can provide to others.

- ❖ Mentor
- ❖ Donate
- ❖ Feed the hungry
- ❖ Donate your product
- ❖ Volunteer your services
- ❖ Make service a company mission

❖ Take advantage of corporate matching programs

BE PATIENT FOR OTHERS

Patience is the ability to stay calm while waiting for an outcome that you need or want. It's a virtue, and there's a reason it's a tough skill to master. Sometimes people can have difficulty understanding things or learning to do something right. Learn to be patient with them. We likely all lose our patience occasionally. But doing so frequently or inappropriately can harm your reputation, damage your relationships, increase stress, or escalate a difficult situation. According to research by psychologist Sarah Schnitker, it comes in three main varieties:

1. Interpersonal patience
2. Life hardship patience
3. Daily hassles patience

Practicing empathy can also enable you to defuse your impatience. Give the other person your full attention and try to see beyond your own frustrations by imagining yourself in the other person's position. Here are four ways to be the patient person you never thought you could be.

❖ Make yourself wait
❖ Relax and take deep breaths
❖ Stop doing things that aren't important
❖ Be mindful of the things making you impatient

HAVING FLEXIBILITY FOR OTHERS

The term flexibility means the ability to bend or adapt to changing forces.

1. Bounce back from setbacks and maintain a positive attitude
2. Adapt to change and new ways of working quickly and easily
3. Shift your priorities in response to the demands of a situation
4. Show willingness to learn new methods, procedures, or techniques
5. Make suggestions for increasing the effectiveness of changes according others plan
6. Look for positive ways to make changes work rather than identifying why change will not work

SAYING THANK YOU TO OTHERS

I'm sure this one seems like common sense, but many people just forget to say thank you, or at least forget how to say it with sincerity. A thank you can be as small as two words or as much as buying someone a gift. Nevertheless, if the action is not done with 100% sincerity, it is wasted. Make sure people know you appreciate them and their efforts. Simply saying it in front of someone else can make a big impact. With the daily pressures on all of us, we often overlook opportunities to thank and compliment the people we are with. Take time to show your appreciation and gratitude to others as they need it. Not only does it make the other person feel better, but you will feel uplifted as well.

Cultivating gratitude doesn't cost any money, and it certainly doesn't take much time, but the benefits are enormous. Research reveals that recognition can benefit both the person who is thanking and who is receiving thanks.

1) Grateful people sleep better
Spending just a few minutes jotting down a few grateful sentiments before bed, and you may sleep better and longer.

2) Gratitude improves self-esteem.
Gratitude increases self-esteem, which is an essential component to everyone for an outstanding performance. It reduces social comparisons.

3) Gratitude improves physical health.
Grateful people experience fewer aches and pains and they report feeling healthier than other people. Not surprisingly, grateful people are also more likely to take care of their health.

4) Gratitude increases mental strength.
Gratitude not only reduces stress, but it may also play a major role in overcoming trauma. According to research, a person with higher levels of gratitude experienced lower rates of post-traumatic stress disorder.

5) Gratitude improves psychological health.
Gratitude reduces a multitude of toxic emotions, ranging from envy and resentment to frustration and regret. Research confirms that gratitude effectively increases happiness and reduces depression.

6) Gratitude opens the door to more relationships.
Not only does saying "thank you" constitute good manners, but showing appreciation can help you win new friends. Research has made it clear that thanking a new acquaintance makes them more likely to seek an ongoing relationship.

7) Gratitude enhances empathy and reduces aggression.
Grateful people are more likely to behave in a prosocial manner, even when others behave less kind.

CONGRATULATING OTHERS ON THEIR SPECIAL EVENTS

If someone does a great job, let them know about it. A big achievement is a perfect chance to remind someone how talented, hard-working, and deserving they are. Offering congratulations is a way of commending someone on achieving a goal or accomplishing something difficult. Let everyone know about it. Openly congratulate someone for a job well done, especially if you're a manager. Your employees will work harder and happier, knowing their manager has mutual respect for them and is willing to express praise and gratitude when deserved. If you know of some inspiring words that would speak to the proud moment and honor your recipient, then quote those inspiring lines when you sign your card. The congratulations card is all about praising someone's achievements, whether it be a personal one like an engagement or a professional one like a promotion. You can also congratulate others on the following events:

- ❖ Newborn
- ❖ Wedding
- ❖ New home
- ❖ Promotion
- ❖ Retirement
- ❖ Graduation

- ❖ Engagements
- ❖ Winning sports
- ❖ Starting a new business
- ❖ Any big accomplishment

COMFORTING SOMEONE IN GRIEF

Often a hug, a helpful hand, a kind word, a listening ear, will go a long way when someone has lost a loved one or suffered some similar loss or tragedy. It can be hard to know how to console a friend or relative who is grieving if it seems that nothing you can do or say help, don't give up. When someone you care about is grieving after a loss, it can be difficult to know what to say. They struggle with many intense and painful emotions, including depression, anger, guilt, and profound sadness. Often, they also feel isolated and alone in their grief, since the intense pain and difficult emotions can make people uncomfortable about offering support. You can't take the pain away, but your presence is more important than it seems. Accept that you can't fix the situation or make your friend or relative feel better. Instead, just be present and offer hope and a positive outlook toward the future.

Recognize that grief is a gradual process. Even small gestures, sending a card or flowers, delivering a meal, helping out with laundry or shopping, or making a regular date to listen and offer support can be a huge source of comfort to a grieving person. You may be afraid of intruding, saying the wrong thing, or making your loved one feel even worse at such a difficult time. Or maybe you think there's little you can do to make things better. That's understandable, but don't let discomfort prevent you from reaching out to someone who is grieving. Now, more than ever, your loved one needs your support. You don't need to have answers or give advice or say and do all the right things. The most important thing you can do for a grieving person is to be there simply. It's your support and caring presence that will help your loved one cope with the pain and gradually heal.

If you are looking for particular words of comfort for someone who is grieving, look no further than within your heart. Forget all clichés between you and other people. It's essential to be genuine. Your goal should be to express compassion, not to cheer up someone who is recently bereaved. You can also help them to take action. If someone in grief seems to be lost, and doesn't know what to do, help them do something. It could be making funeral arrangements, and it could be making a doctor's appointment; it could be making phone calls. Don't do it all yourself. Let them take action too because it helps in the healing process.

The keys to helping a loved one who's grieving

- ❖ Offer to help in practical ways
- ❖ Maintain your support after the funeral
- ❖ Let your grieving loved one know that you're there to listen
- ❖ Understand that everyone grieves differently and for different lengths of time
- ❖ Don't let fears about saying or doing the wrong thing stop you from reaching out

VOLUNTEERING FOR DIFFERENT EVENTS

Community service is one of the best ways to improve the lives of others. Donating your time allows you to connect with your community and make it a better place. Volunteer work is also flexible: You can participate as much as your schedule allows, and you can choose opportunities that fit your interests and hobbies. The possibilities are endless:

- ❖ Help at a food bank.
- ❖ Teach someone a skill.
- ❖ Volunteer at a local school.
- ❖ Clean up a local park or beach
- ❖ Aid a local animal shelter or retirement home.

Volunteering is an activity where an individual or group freely gives time to benefit another person, group, or organization. Volunteering is also renowned for skill development and promotes goodness or to improve human quality of life. Volunteering can help you make friends, learn new skills, advance your career, and even feel happier and healthier. However, the benefits of volunteering can be enormous. Volunteering offers vital help to people in need, worthwhile causes, and the community, but the benefits can be even greater for you, the volunteer. Volunteering is one of the most amazing things you can do. It not only befits others; it has also benefited yourself. Benefits of volunteering:

- ❖ Volunteering connects you to others
- ❖ Volunteering can advance your career
- ❖ Volunteering is good for your mind and body
- ❖ Volunteering brings fun and fulfillment to your life

DONATING SOMETHING TO CHARITY

Giving charity helps needy people a lot. Donating to charity is a major mood-booster. The knowledge that you're helping others is hugely empowering and, in turn, can make you feel happier and more fulfilled. Having the power to improve others' lives is, to many people, a privilege, and one that comes with its sense of obligation. There are lots of ways to donate to charities online or in your local community. Instead of buying yourself a new gadget or outfit, spend that money more positively. Donating to the causes you care about benefits the charities themselves, but it can also be deeply rewarding for you. Millions of people give charity regularly to support the causes they believe in and the positive effect it has on their own lives. Your donations can inspire your nearest and dearest to give to causes important to them. They could even bring about a family-wide effort to back a charity or charities that have special significance to you. There are many positive effects of donating money to charity.

1. Help others in need
2. Get a tax deduction
3. Experience more pleasure
4. Give, If You Can't Volunteer
5. Motivate friends and family
6. Bring more meaning to your life
7. Realize that every little bit helps
8. Promote generosity in your children
9. Improve personal money management

STOP AND HELP THE NEEDY

Let's suppose you are on the road, and there is an older man who is blind and needs someone to help him cross the road. Here is the time for you to get into it, to help that person. Sometimes all they need is a push or the use of your cell phone. You must be ready to help with such needs, and you must not leave someone helpless when you can afford what they need.

Remember that You reap what you sow. You eventually have to face up to the consequences of your actions. This is life, and we don't know what's going to happen to us in the future. Maybe in the future, you are that older adult who needs help, and no one is ready to help you. No need to worry, now you have time you can make your future. You can guide your siblings, friends, and relatives. You can advise them to share these points with others. In this way, you can make your society better.

TEACHING GOOD THINGS TO OTHERS

Take the time to teach someone a skill you know. For example, teaching your old grandfather to use a mobile, laptop, or any social media, teaching your child to ride a bike, teaching your co-worker a valuable computer skill, etc.

Teachers often dream about having a classroom of students looking to help them and help each other. The good news is you can develop a classroom of service-minded students who want to help others and make their schools and communities better. You can develop skills like caring, giving, and helping among your students, or anyone. Everyone in this world is busy learning. You don't have to go to school for education. You can learn about the reality of life from your observation and experiences.

HELPING AND CARING FOR POOR PEOPLE

Some people have much more than they need to live, while others have barely enough to survive. Be respectful and friendly to these people because nobody becomes poor out of desire. Maybe you live life lavishly. You do not only enjoy the joy of essentials but also have what you want and desire, a luxurious living providing you extra comfort. On the other hand, some people cannot even afford the basic requirements of life. They do not have shelter to live, food to eat, and clothes to wear. It's their fortune that they have nothing for them. They didn't choose to be poor; maybe some tragedy happened that caused them to lose everything. Change your perspective. Instead of considering them as a project to help, view them as people to love and respect.

Poor people do not have enough clothing, food, education, and healthcare. Poverty is a result of economic, political, and social deprivation. They have inadequate nutrition, higher risk of diseases, and lack access to healthcare and essentials for living, resulting in low achievement. You cannot make such people opulent but can at least help them achieve the essentials of life and lead a prosperous life. Caring for the poor and needy people is a noble endeavor. The more you give to the poor and needy people, the more you strengthen their dependency. If you provide them with the chance or opportunity, you'll see an effective and long-lasting improvement.

Create a new system built on inter-dependency, which motivates them to work and move forward, and their dignity is maintained. Tossing out money or other kinds of donation do help the poor and needy people. Still, the need is to direct your energies and efforts in raising them, building relationships, teaching them, and regaining their self-confidence and self-esteem to work for themselves. You have a chance to start to give them your monthly gift. Monthly giving is the perfect way to help our poorest brothers and sisters. By setting up an automatic monthly donation, you can direct your funds to a specific area. Remember, providing employment opportunities of all kinds by the responsible government agencies in the

State contributes to helping the poor raise their standard of living. You can give them;

- ❖ Clothes
- ❖ Education
- ❖ Fund raising
- ❖ Collection drive
- ❖ Donate groceries
- ❖ Give eatables things
- ❖ Personal financial help
- ❖ Donate old belongings
- ❖ Group involvement/volunteering team

HELP SOMEONE WHO IS ON THE EDGE

When you suspect someone is having a nervous breakdown, you must take it very seriously. A nervous breakdown may cause an individual to stop normal functioning, as well as an array of other side effects. You must understand what a nervous breakdown is, the early warning signs, and how to help someone having a nervous breakdown. One of the most frightening experiences a person can have is hearing a friend or loved one say they want to die. If someone is suicidal, urge them to get help. If they don't, call a suicide hotline or doctor yourself to get advice. Being available for them to discuss their thoughts and feelings is often a sanctuary for them. Remind your loved one that you are no more than a phone call away, and that you'll be there for them no matter the time. Even though they may have a difficult time expressing it, they appreciate and love you beyond comprehension.

If you come across a person who is committing suicide, it is important to manage it carefully. Introduce yourself and try to establish trust with that person using an empathic approach that does not make the suicidal person feel powerless or overwhelmed. Find out how you can help; ask if they would like to speak with a therapist or relative. Try to maintain a continuous conversation and relate to the person's experience. Do not engage in tricks or reverse psychology. Work towards allowing the person to emerge from the situation without losing face. Always be mindful of your physical safety. Unfortunately, sometimes a suicidal person is lost despite all possible efforts. This can be very distressing, and you must seek help if you are having trouble coping with a trauma that you have encountered during these situations. If it is safe, you may also drive that person to the emergency room. Doctors will assess their mental and physical health and create a clear plan to keep them safe. If, on the other hand, you believe the threat is serious, but not imminent, it's still important to act, but you may take the time to show support, listen, and encourage them to seek professional help. Help is available. Here are some helpful tips you can use in these situations.

1. *Show openness:* Be sympathetic, non-judgmental, patient, calm, and accepting. The person will pick up on your attitude and begin to mirror it for themselves.

2. *Show support:* There are a number of different things you can do to be a supportive and empathetic friend. The key is to avoid being judgmental or dismissive of what your friend is feeling.

3. *Speak from the heart:* There are no right or wrong things you can say if you are speaking out of love and concern. Just be yourself. Show that you care by talking to them, holding them while they cry, or whatever else is necessary.

4. *Listen:* A suicidal person usually is carrying around some burden that they feel they just can't handle anymore. Offer to listen as they vent their feelings of despair, anger, and loneliness. Sometimes this is enough to lighten the load just enough for them to carry on.

HELPING SOMEONE TO GET ACTIVE

It's also another way to help others. A person in your life who wants to get healthy might need a helping hand. Offer to go walking, running, or join a gym together. Once they get started, they can have profound effects. Lots of people struggle to get enough physical activity. If someone you care about is having a hard time getting active, you can help. Here are some tips to get you started.

1. Choose healthy gifts

For birthdays or special occasions, choose gifts that encourage your loved one to be more active.

2. Be understanding

What are the other one's reasons for not being more active? Maybe he or she feels overwhelmed or embarrassed. Ask what you can do to be supportive.

3. Recognize small efforts

You have to be patient and point out positive choices. Remember, any amount of physical activity is better than none! Offer encouragement and praise to others.

4. Make their regular routine

Advise them to pick a certain time for physical activity, like right after your favorite TV show.

5. Suggest activities you can do together

Start small. Learn new stretches and warm-up exercises. Join a fitness class with them just to show that you are with them. Choose an activity that's new for both of you.

MAKING FEEL OTHERS THAT YOU ARE HERE TO LISTEN THEM

We all require self-focus. Listening, not talking, is the most important part of communicating. When you deeply understand what other people are saying, you build the foundation for an intelligent and meaningful conversation and an intimate relationship. When you listen superficially, you lay the groundwork for a shallow discussion, one likely to frustrate both of you. You leave that person feeling misunderstood and alone. Often someone sad, depressed, angry, or frustrated just needs someone who will listen. Venting and talking through an issue is a huge help. So, give your best to understand what someone thinks and feels to enter his or her world, to see through his or her eyes. It takes a lot of concentration and determination to be an active listener. Old habits are hard to break, and if your listening skills are as bad, then you have to do a lot of work to break these bad habits. Listening to another person can be valuable at any time, especially when we realize how rewarding it is for the other person to get the kind of respect listening communicates. Yet there are certain times when listening is a particularly valuable interpersonal action to take.

❖ When you want to build goodwill. When you listen to another you speak interest, affection, and respect. You thereby create the trust and goodwill that will predictably come back to you.

❖ To find a solution to a problem that works for both parties, each person must not only understand their win, but the win of the other person as well. The only way to understand the other person's win is to listen.

❖ When we are not sure we understand what another thinks or feels. Unless we shut our mouth and open our ears, we can never get the information we need to understand what we don't know.

❖ When the other person doesn't feel understood. When a person doesn't feel understood, he or she will react with at least frustration and perhaps even with anger and resentment. Better to listen at these times so that the other person feels understood, keeping an eye on the big picture rather than the immediate moment.

❖ When the other person is upset. An upset person will predictably find it difficult to communicate and cooperate with you. Helping this person defuse their upset by listening to them has the power to gain unity in the problem-solving process. This process serves to garner the goodwill that often translates into warmth and friendship.

Hear What People Are Really Saying
Listening is one of the most important skills you can have. How well you listen has a major impact on your job effectiveness and your relationships with others. There are many key techniques you can use to develop your active listening skills:

1. Defer judgment
2. Provide feedback
3. Respond appropriately
4. Show that you're listening
5. Ask open-ended questions
6. Monitor your intensity level
7. Pay attention to the other person
8. Paraphrase what other people say
9. Avoid focusing on what you will say
10. Speak respectfully when you disagree
11. Watch your nonverbal communication

12. Encourage people to express their feelings
13. Let someone finish talking before you speak
14. Give others time to think before they speak
15. Do not ask a question, then answer it yourself
16. Ask for feedback if someone is distant or upset
17. Respond to criticism without getting defensive

Start using these active listening techniques to become a better communicator, improve workplace productivity, and develop better relationships. So, by listening rather than talking, you give something valuable to the person who's speaking. Especially if you are taking in what that person is saying and not thinking about something else, the speaker will appreciate that gift, and you will have created a bond. He or she will feel understood and validated. It's a powerful relationship-building tool and an especially powerful sales tool.

HAVING ABILITY TO ACCEPT OTHERS AS THEY ARE

Despite their personality traits not being how we'd like or wish; we cannot love people and expect them to change just for us. Loving others with the expectation that things should go our way is not a reflection of love, but a sign of control or the need to fix others, manifesting as codependency. Practicing non-judgment of others gives ourselves and others the freedom to be themselves. In accepting others, we become more truthful in accepting the reality of the moment, of their potential and our connection to all of the above as an act of love. Acceptance is the ability to see that others have a right to be their unique persons. That means having a right to their feelings, thoughts, and opinions. When you accept people for who they are, you let go of your desire to change them. You make them feel the way they want to feel, and you allow them to be and think differently from you. Everyone is different in one way or another. Once you understand this truth, you can stop trying to change them into the people you want them to be and start accepting them for who they are. Acceptance of others' feelings is not easy when people act differently than we do. We all have trouble accepting those who are different. Here are some ways to take others as they are.

1. Look for positivity

Not accepting others is a result of seeing the negative in them. Instead of focusing on why someone is different, focus on their strengths. Stop judging yourself. Our judgments of others are often a result of our criticisms. If you stop putting pressure on yourself to do things the "right" way, you'll also stop putting pressure on others.

2. Focus on the now

A lack of acceptance can generate from comparing things to the past. So, think about the future. Comparing items to the past always hinders the recognition of what is.

3. Try not to compare

The key to accepting people as they are is learning not to compare. Trying to compare one unique person to another is like trying to compare apples to oranges. Unfortunately, we all do it. We compare ourselves to others, and we compare other people to some standard because there is always going to be someone better, smarter, or richer. Instead, we must accept that each person is on a different path in life.

4. Give thoughtful advice

Have you ever tried to talk to other people about your problems, only to have them give you terrible advice in return? They respond in a way that makes you wonder if they were even listening to anything you said! Those people probably were looking, but they failed to put much thought into their responses. Or, they let their feelings get in the way of yours. To show empathy, you must learn to give advice in a way that is in line with other people's' unique feelings, characteristics, and personalities.

5. Allow others to be different

How boring would life be if everyone was the same as everyone else in the world? If everyone looked the same, had the same personality, the same interests, and experiences, we would lose interest in other people pretty quickly. Luckily, each of us has a unique set of qualities and characteristics that make us different. Even though we know that these differences are for the best, sometimes we feel uncomfortable with them. We either try to change people who are different, or we avoid or ignore them. This is their right, and we are no one to change them.

6. Avoid right/wrong dichotomies

It's tempting to see the world in black and white with a right and wrong way to do things, but that's just not how it is. Items don't have to be right or wrong if you choose to accept them as they are.

7. Watch your thoughts and be non-judgmental

You have to do your best to push your thoughts in a non-judgmental and more accepting direction. It's easy to look at others and point out their flaws. Sometimes we judge and criticize people without even realizing it. The more challenging and empathetic response would be to point out the good in each person. When we accept others as they are, we understand that they are doing the best that they can do at the time. Remember, if they could do any better, they would.

8. Don't try to control the feelings of others
With feelings, there is no right or wrong answer. Instead of trying to control or change other people's' feelings, you must accept their feelings. We must allow people to have feelings without telling them how they should feel. Empathetic people understand that feelings are difficult to control and accept people's' feelings for what they are. So, have let them do what they want.

GIVING GIFTS TO OTHERS WHICH YOU CAN AFFORD

As you know very well, we have a culture where people have easy access to material goods and anything that they want, and they already have enough of or too much. But what is difficult to do yet really precious to some people is to do something that makes the other person happy. Sometimes you pick out a gift that you just know is very thoughtful, and the other person is going to love it, and you are considering that it's going to fill a gap. Yes, it works. It makes another person feel that they are important for you. It creates a healthier environment between two people. People feel secure and come to that that there is someone who cares about them and is you. They respect you more. The main purpose is to become more respectful, and it's indeed to make them happy. To make them feel that you have something for them that makes the other person more comfortable. Science says giving gifts makes you happier than receiving them, so the process of giving gifts to others has also benefits for yourself like:

- ❖ Giving is contagious
- ❖ Giving evokes gratitude
- ❖ Giving makes us feel happy
- ❖ Giving is good for our health
- ❖ Giving promotes cooperation
- ❖ Giving promotes social connection

HAVING ABILITY TO SHIFT OTHERS ATTITUDE TOWARDS POSITIVE ATTITUDE

With the help of a positive attitude, you inspire others. It helps them to get a more positive attitude towards life. With the help of personal development and self-growth, people can make decisions better and adapt to any type of challenge. When a person focuses on a positive attitude, he plans and utilizes his time correctly. Therefore, a positive attitude not only improves the skills but also helps the person create a positive attitude towards life and a very major benefit for their life. Because a person determines to learn will fail multiple times while learning, but he will never give up on learning. A positive attitude has many more major benefits on life like it helps their talent shines. The genius of a person goes waste if not recognized with constant practice and efforts for improvement. With a positive attitude, a person can improve his ability and feel confident to show his expertise to the world. Have a positive attitude and share it with others.

There will be tough times in life. When these tough times occur, they need to have the skills and attributes to deal effectively with them. A positive attitude cannot prevent bad things from happening, but it will help them deal with them. They will have greater confidence, resilience, personal and interpersonal skills to cope with any eventuality. A positive attitude cannot make all their life experiences positive. There will always be times when bad things happen. Often, these events will occur due to circumstances beyond their control; other times, they will screw up and create a bit of a mess for themselves. When they develop a positive attitude, they learn that they can change just about any circumstance in their life. If they can't change the situation, you can change their attitude towards the experience, which makes it less unpleasant. Knowing all this allows them to stay calm, composed, and in control when a crisis strikes. You can then determine the best course of action to take. That will enable them to minimize the damage caused by the negative experience. A positive attitude is not just about improving their life by helping them do and have more of what they want from life. It improves their life by assisting them to deal better with negative experiences too. It all depends upon you that how you shift their attitude towards positivity.

HOW TO BE A MORE CREATIVE TOWARDS YOUR GOAL

Creativity isn't something people are born with; it's a skill that can be learned. The brain is like a muscle that needs to be developed in this case, using cognitive exercises. Everyone has the ways they like to "get in shape. Of all human activities, creativity comes closest to providing the fulfillment we all hope to get. Creativity allows us to stretch out minds, do new and exciting things, and engage ourselves in a way that takes us closer to reaching our full potential. So, what is it exactly that makes a person creative? Are some people just born that way, or is it a skill that you can develop much like a muscle? Some people possess what he refers to as a creative personality. While some people indeed come by these tendencies naturally, incorporating a few of these artistic practices into your daily life might just help you achieve your full creative potential.

We all had those frustrating moments when we have to come up with a brilliant new idea, but no matter how much we squint at our computer screens, we just can't seem to think of anything good. But it may be that we're looking at it wrong. What can we do to exercise that creative muscle when we're struggling to develop new ideas? Here are some different ways to improve your creative thinking.

SOME WAYS TO JUMPSTART YOUR CREATIVITY

* Start with writing
* Take a creative course
* Channel your inner child
* Travelling to some places
* Brainstorming during exercise
* Connect with creative people
* Listen to music when working
* Take breaks after every workday
* unwind of watching funny content

1) Start With Writing

One way to refocus is by doing a morning free write. Research has proved that regular workplace journaling allows you to rediscover your perspective and become more productive. Instead of jumping right into your projects when you get into the office, block off ten minutes for writing and get a notebook and paper just to write. Writing in a more free-form style will allow your creative juices to flow, while also forcing you to put your thoughts into written words.

2) *Take A Creative Course*

If you're the kind of person who prefers guided instruction, taking a creative course could be the right way to direct your creativity. Creative courses could be anything from creative writing to photo and video to music, art, and design. Regardless of which route you take, you'll be exposed to different ways of thinking and approaches to working that you can apply to your work. It may help you uncover some of your strengths and work on your weaknesses. By sharing your ideas with others, you are forced to find ways to formulate your thoughts into words and visuals, while learning to handle critique from others. It'll also surround you with other people who share the goal of developing their creative skills. If you feel like you lack direction in your thinking, it is advantageous to you.

3) *Channel Your Inner Child*

Most importantly, have fun with your work. A child sees everything as an adventure and makes the most of every moment. Instead of being concerned about your responsibilities, focus all of your energy into one project at a time so you can put your best foot forward. Children are considered as naturally creative because they know no limits to their creativity. Instead of being concerned or self-conscious that your work isn't good enough, be willing to take risks to push your creative limits.

4) Travelling To Some Places

Since your creativity is related to how your brain works, it's essential to keep your mind stimulated by new sights, sounds, tastes, smells, and experiences. Expose yourself to an entirely different point of view through a unique cultural experience. Keeping your sense sharp allows the synapses in your brain to think in new ways. The importance of going to different places is essential as other points as it leads you towards creativity. When you visit new areas, new things and ideas come to your mind. By engaging with the local art and people, you allow yourself to learn new ways of thinking that you can later apply to your ideas.

5) Brainstorming During Exercise

If you feel like you're working your brain hard and still coming out empty-handed, try pushing yourself physically for thirty minutes. Research shows that exercise can be linked to more creative thinking. Much more of the brain is devoted to movement than to language. You must take thirty minutes out of your time for exercise. It'll benefit both your body and mind.

6) Connect With Creative People

When you've hit a wall with your ideas, it may be time to tap into others' creativity. Surrounding yourself with people with whom you can share and get feedback on your thoughts and opinions is good for your creativity, it's good for your career. These different points of view can be a fresh perspective on a project you've been staring at for too long. Not only can creative people give you feedback on your projects, but their drivers will also keep you motivated to do your best work. If you surround yourself with like-minded people, you could fall into the trap of confirmation bias, where you never see the faults in your job because everyone agrees with you. To start networking with other creative minds, you can explore people's work on different platforms.

7) Listen To Music While Working

Listening to music can help you focus on whatever task you're currently doing. It can also put you in a better mood, and even calm your nerves if you're feeling anxious. Certain forms of music can help channel your creativity better than others and tune out the office's noises. While music with extreme changes of pace or lyrics can be distracting, ambient music can help increase processing levels and promote creative thinking.

8) *Take Breaks After Every Workday*

If a large project seems overwhelming, make a step-by-step plan. Focus on one manageable step at a time, rather than taking on everything at once. Breaks allow your mind to continue to work on these ideas without getting stuck in a funk where you can't organize your thoughts. Make sure to allow yourself to block off designated break sessions in your calendar, so you don't lose that time after being scheduled for endless, back-to-back meetings.

9) *Unwind Of Watching Funny Content*

Have you hit the point in your creativity block where you're spending hours watching your favorite cartoons etc. Research shows there's a strong correlation between humor and creativity. A laugh can bring you closer to those moments of inspiration. Humor also puts you in a better mood, allowing you to think more freely and solve creative problems better. If you look at your project from a more lighthearted perspective, you'll have a fresh perspective on the issue.

CHARACTERISTICS OF CREATIVE PEOPLE

- ❖ Creative people are smart.
- ❖ Creative people are disciplined.
- ❖ Creative people are energetic, but focused.
- ❖ Creative people are conservative, yet rebellious.
- ❖ Creative people are passionate, but objective about their work.
- ❖ Creative people are sensitive and open to experience, but happy and joyful.
- ❖ Creative people are realistic dreamers, creative people are extroverted and introverted.

CONCLUSION

Helping others is a great way to spread joy to others and get the most out of life. You have something for everyone, something for your parents, your kids, your husband/wife, your company, your friends, and society. You have to find what you have and whom it belongs to. Just being available makes their world go beautiful. You have so much for everyone. Your time, your advice, your services, your kindness are all considered giving. These all add significant value to your account because you have a lot of things for everyone. Pay attention to the people around you and what you can do to make their lives a little easier. An act of kindness, any simple gesture can improve someone's day. Being friendly and thoughtful can make a huge difference, and maintaining good relationships is good for your heart.

Enjoy reading the eBook.

Thanks

REFERENCES:

1. https://www.wikihow.com/Be-Loyal
2. https://zenhabits.net/25-ways-to-help-a-fellow-human-being-today/
3. https://examples.yourdictionary.com/examples-of-personality-traits.html
4. https://www.verywellmind.com/top-reasons-to-smile-every-day-2223755
5. https://www.mindtools.com/CommSkll/ActiveListening.htm
6. https://www.dougbrittonbooks.com/onlinebiblestudies-relationships-friendsfamilywork/listencarefullytodeeplyunderstand-t25-2/
7. https://www.energize.com/the-benefits-of-encouragement/
8. https://www.helpguide.org/articles/grief/helping-someone-who-is-grieving.htm
9. https://www.helpguide.org/articles/healthy-living/volunteering-and-its-surprising-benefits.htm
10. https://www.thelifeyoucansave.org/blog/9-positive-effects-of-donating-money-to-charity/
11. https://medium.com/the-mvp/know-yourself-know-your-worth-self-awareness-how-well-do-you-know-yourself-386beeef503f
12. https://ozobot.com/blog/how-teachers-can-make-students-aware-of-their-capacity-to-help-others
13. https://www.health.harvard.edu/mind-and-mood/ways-to-support-someone-who-is-grieving
14. https://www.linkedin.com/pulse/20140827214710-141895933-top-10-ways-to-help-poor-and-needy-people

15. https://www.postable.com/blog/11-reasons-to-send-a-congratulations-card/

16. https://www.psychologytoday.com/us/blog/happiness-purpose/201406/happiness-others-8-listen-listen-listen

17. https://ifightdepression.com/en/community-professionals/police/approaching-a-person-on-the-edge

18. https://www.verywellmind.com/what-to-do-when-a-friend-is-suicidal-1065472

19. https://www.rehabspot.com/treatment/spiritual/love-for-others/

20. https://www.bastiansolutions.com/blog/5-easy-ways-to-show-people-respect-and-gratitude/

21. https://www.forbes.com/sites/amymorin/2014/11/23/7-scientifically-proven-benefits-of-gratitude-that-will-motivate-you-to-give-thanks-year-round/#76d2bc7183c0

22. https://www.happify.com/hd/forgiving-others-is-the-best-thing-you-can-do-for-yourself/

23. https://www.psychologytoday.com/us/blog/mindful-anger/201409/how-do-you-forgive-even-when-it-feels-impossible-part-1

24. https://montessorirocks.org/10-ways-to-show-compassion/

25. https://www.conovercompany.com/empathy-accept-others-for-who-they-are/

26. https://www.positivelypresent.com/2011/11/what-if-you-accepted-people-just-as-they-are.html

27. https://elementalwellnesscoaching.wordpress.com/2013/06/14/10-benefits-of-being-honest/

28. https://www.theladders.com/career-advice/how-to-upgrade-your-mindset-for-success
https://www.skillsyouneed.com/ps/mindsets.html